The Emotional Pain Diagram

An Explanation of How the Different
Feelings and Emotions Develop and Progress,
Leading to a Diagnosis of Mental Illness

Ty C. Colbert, Ph.D.

KEVCO PUBLISHING

ORANGE, CALIFORNIA

Copyright © 2016 Kevco Publishing
1335 N. Sarita Pl.
Orange, CA 92869

TYCO33@aol.com

Printed in the United States of America

The author has made every effort to use sources believed to be reliable to provide information that is accurate and compatible with the standards generally accepted at the time of publication. Because medical and psychological science is continually advancing, our knowledge base continues to expand. Therefore, as new information becomes available, changes in procedures become necessary. We recommend that the reader always consult current research and specific institutional policies before performing any clinical procedure. The author and publisher shall not be liable for any special, consequential, or exemplary damages resulting, in whole or in part, from the readers' use of, or reliance on, the information contained in this book. The publisher has no responsibility for the persistence or accuracy of URLs for external or third-party Internet websites referred to in this publication and does not guarantee.

Colbert, Ty C.
ISBN 978-0-9891607-5-9

1. Mental illness 2. Emotional healing 3. Feelings and emotions

AUTHOR OF

Healing Runaway Minds
How to Understand and Recover From
Major Mental Disorders with Special
Emphasis on "Schizophrenia"

Schizophrenia-Simply Understood
Developing the Basis for a Correct
Understanding, Healing,
and Recovery Model

Breakdown To Breakthrough
A Workbook on How to Recover
and Grow From a Diagnosis
of "Schizophrenia"

*It is strongly recommended
that suffering individuals
and their helpers enlist the services of a
licensed mental health professional
while reading and/or performing the
exercises in this book.*

The Emotional Pain Diagram

INTRODUCTION

BELOW YOU WILL FIND A FIGURE of what I have labeled as the Emotional Pain Diagram, with each symbol or letter defined accordingly.

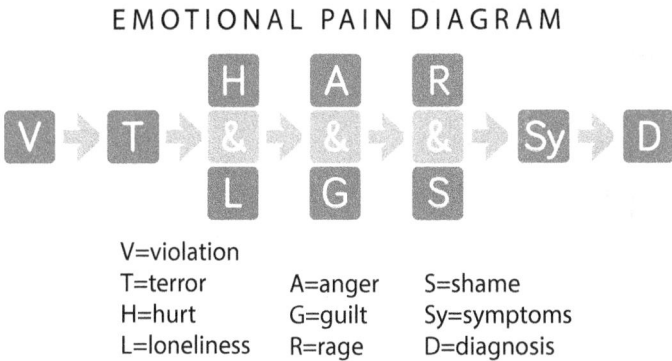

EMOTIONAL PAIN DIAGRAM

V=violation
T=terror   A=anger   S=shame
H=hurt   G=guilt   Sy=symptoms
L=loneliness   R=rage   D=diagnosis

It may be best for me to first share with you how this diagram came about before I explain it.

HOW AND WHY THE DIAGRAM WAS DEVELOPED

I first received a bachelor's degree in Mechanical Engineering. After a few years working as an engineer, I realized that I much preferred working with people. As a result of this new awareness, I decided to become a high school teacher. After a few more years, I finally chose to become a psychologist.

Since I was already enrolled at the University of Southern California working on my state teaching credential, I decided to look around at USC for a doctoral program in counseling or psychology. Just by chance, the school of education also had a counseling department. So the switch to this department was as easy as simply signing up for the appropriate classes.

To my pleasant surprise, the counseling department was not set up to prepare individuals for counseling in a school setting as much as it was to prepare individuals for private practice. I don't know all the details, but when one professor in particular was hired on, he changed the program to better fit students wishing to enter private practice. In any case, the curriculum was perfect for me because private practice was my ultimate goal.

In addition, the program was as intense as any that I have seen or heard about from individuals who attended other graduate programs. The challenge was not in the academic or didactic aspect, but the actual hands-on practicum work. To get through the program each student had to take a series of five practicum classes, including one in which the student participated as a student instructor.

Each class consisted of ten students, one professor and one or two student instructors. For the first part of the class, each student counseled someone who had come to the student clinic seeking help. While you were counseling, several of your fellow classmates and instructors would observe you through a one-way mirror. After counseling two individuals each class, the whole class would then meet together, at which point your counseling sessions would be openly critiqued.

The critiquing process for all of us, which at times lasted past midnight, was not abusive, but it could be quite confrontational at times. The department was committed to making sure each future counselor could perform at a doctoral level. Consequently, the pass rate for the first time through the first of the five courses was about 30% or three out of ten. The class was graded on either a pass or no-pass level so your grade did not affect your GPA.

I failed to pass the first time and here is why. I grew up in a family that did not express any feelings other than occasional anger. We were never physically or emotionally abused by our parents, nor did we as siblings physically fight each other. But we would suppress our anger and then explode verbally at times.

I actually made it all the way through this first basic counseling class, but received a no-pass grade. On my second try, I made it to the third week, at which point a different instructor told me I should drop out of the program for a while and obtain some personal counseling. So, in a sense, I was kicked out of the program because I was not ready for it.

After some therapy with an excellent therapist who had graduated from the program, I felt I was ready for my third try. I did make it through, but just barely. Yet it was this third class that changed my life, eventually leading to the development of the Emotional Pain Diagram.

At the time, I had a lot of personal issues going on in my life and, as before, I had suppressed a lot of anger. In the third week of the class, with all ten students in one room in a circle to critique our individual sessions, the instructor asked me what I was angry about. I told him that I was not angry because I was not aware of any anger. He then had everyone in the class share how they were perceiving me. All nine of them, plus the student instructor, shared that not only did I look like I was ready to explode, but that I scared some of them with my hidden anger.

Since I was not aware of any anger, I quickly denied it and thought they were all wrong. In fact, some degree of paranoia slipped into my thoughts. I began to think that they were lying for some reason, perhaps to get me out of the program.

Then, two days later while driving in my car, I suddenly became aware of what I was angry about. At that point I knew they were right and I felt like a fool. And, of course, I had to share this truth to the class.

Then in another two weeks or so, the same situation occurred in the class, with me again believing that they were all wrong, this time for sure. But on the way home, while in my car, it again dawned on me that they were right. So I told myself that at least I was making some progress. This time it didn't take me two days to become aware.

But as an ex-engineer, and a person who needs control over his life, the blocking out of certain feelings greatly disturbed me. As a consequence, I went to work to figure out what I needed to do, not only to become aware of my feelings, but to correctly understand and manage them. To do so, I spent considerable time attempting to become aware of myself at the deepest level.

I also had a couple of clients who were keenly and accurately aware of their feelings. I quizzed them over and over, probably learning more from them than they were learning from me. Actually, learning together is quite common in the counseling profession.

One client in particular, a very bright nine-year-old who had been abused and had to become extremely perceptive to survive, taught me as much as anyone. The following are a few lines of an ongoing dialogue that I had with her while she was in therapy with me and another female therapist who specializes with children who have been seriously abused. The full account of this dialogue can be found in Chapter Eleven of my book *Healing Runaway Minds*. Notice the central focus on her feelings.

Betty: I want to hurt myself.

Ty: Why?

Betty: To push down my anger towards my daddy. He hurt me real bad.

Ty: What are the feelings you are trying to push down?

Betty: My anger, hurt, and loneliness.

Ty: What happens when all the hurt comes up?

Betty: I feel real alone.

Ty: So the loneliness comes up, too?

Betty: Yes, then I feel cold inside.

Ty: You don't like those feelings?

Betty: No, I try to push them back down.

Ty: How do you try to push the feelings down?

Betty: I bite myself.

Ty: How does that push the feelings down?

Betty: 'Cause I get mad at me.

Ty: How does anger push down feelings of loneliness?

Betty: When I'm angry, I don't feel quite as alone. My anger is easier to feel and blocks out the loneliness.

Ty: Do you feel more important when you're angry?

Betty: Yes.

Ty: Is that because the person who has hurt you has made you feel worthless?

Betty: Small.

Ty: When you were close to death, did you feel cut off from everyone?

Betty: Yes.

Ty: Why was that so hard?

Betty: Because nobody in the whole world cared for me.

Ty: How did that make you feel?

Betty: Like I was no good.

Ty: Can you describe the feelings?

Betty: Cold and real alone, and bad, like I wasn't worth anything at all. It's the worst feeling I ever had.

Ty: What else were you aware of?

Betty: How much I really needed somebody.

Ty: You absolutely believed that nobody loved you and that's why you tried to kill yourself?

Betty: Yes.

She does not use the terms "rage" or "shame" specifically, but you will notice them in the dialogue in the form of anger toward herself and the use of such terms as "worthless" and "no good." She also did not use the word "terror," but used the term "coldness" instead. All of us experience terror at times. With extreme cases of abuse and loneliness, children especially will often experience an element of coldness instead.

As a result of my personal embarrassment at USC and personal tutoring from a few insightful individuals (mostly ones who had been seriously abused as children), the Emotional Pain Diagram eventually unfolded. In fact, the more I correctly understood my feelings, and those of others, the more I began to realize that a very particular and precise sequence takes place leading to a so-called major mental illness condition. Thus, with this background, allow me to explain each step in the process.

STEP 1: VIOLATION (V) AND TERROR (T)

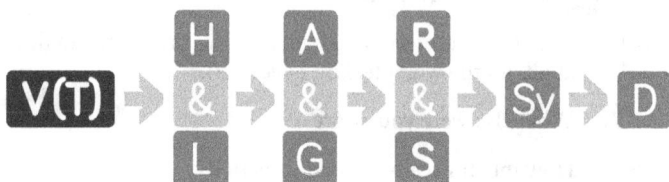

V(T) → H & L → A & G → R & S → Sy → D

As conscious individuals, we cannot help but choose, and as we make choices, we invest a part of who we are into that choice. Once we have made a choice (consciously or unconsciously), and now have a personal investment in that choice, we automatically make ourselves available to the affirmation or disaffirmation of others.

For example, let's say that Johnny, age 12, is getting ready for school and to do so he opens up his closet and pulls down a certain shirt to wear. Even though he may have only taken a second to choose, he did choose and did so for some reason. Even if his mother tells him what shirt to wear, he is still making a choice to go along with her recommendation.

Later at school, by wearing that shirt, he is now vulnerable to the affirmation or disaffirmation of his peers. If he is affirmed for that shirt, he will feel a warm sensation run through his body. He may not consciously be aware of this warm sensation, but it will be there in some form or degree.

But what if his peers, or one influential person in particular, chooses to make fun of him and his shirt in front of his peers? Johnny may be able to laugh off the incident, but most likely he will feel hurt and alone, and likely not want to wear that shirt again.

Regardless of how he may or may not have reacted, he will feel violated (V) at some point because he or his selfhood or his choice was attacked. Once again, he may not be consciously or fully aware, as I was not with my anger, but the violation is felt at some level. He also will need to attempt to suppress as much of the awareness as possible, perhaps laughing off the incident, in order to not appear as if he had been emotionally injured. Yet, perhaps back at his home, the results of this violation may surface in the form of anger at a sibling or parent.

In summary, as conscious human beings, we make choices and then consequently become emotionally vulnerable to those choices. Even with a newborn infant, at some level of awareness there will be a choice made in the infant's effort to bond with the mother. Therefore, we cannot help but make ourselves vulnerable to the often intentional violations by others. And as you will soon see, it is these violations that, as they add up, result in the symptoms used to diagnose someone as mentally ill. For example, hallucinations are usually created by the mind of the person to help manage a series of violations.

In addition, an element of terror can and often does accompany the violating aspects of the equation. For example, the other day as I was driving along, a policeman just happened to pull out and follow me for a couple of blocks before turning onto a side street. Even though I was almost certain that I had not broken the law, the longer he followed me, the more I felt a growing element of terror.

Jokingly, I had to ask myself, "What was that terror about?" After all, at the moment all that I would be guilty of was a small traffic fine, and as far as I could tell, I was driving within the law.

The terror was the result of past events when a person with authority had power over me and could or did harm me. Even though my life has been a relatively safe one, there have been moments when I have been in a position where I was violated and had no ability or power to protect myself. For example, I remember one time at a bus stop when an older kid hit me in the stomach, embarrassing me in front of my peers. Even though that happened about 60 years ago, I can still imagine or even feel some of the terror involved.

I am sure that the bus stop incident did not necessarily specifically cause the terror to surface as the policeman pulled in behind me. But I am aware that such terror moments result in our bodies and minds quickly taking off, trying to build a defense or wall against that terror. I can only imagine what it must be like for a child to be raped or subjected to a raging parent. In fact, those individuals who have come to understand such conditions as schizophrenia from a violational basis identify terror as the true origin of the resulting symptoms.

In closing, who has not been subjected to hundreds of such violations, many that we actually do to ourselves through self-criticism and poor choices?

STEP 2: HURT (H) AND LONELINESS (L)

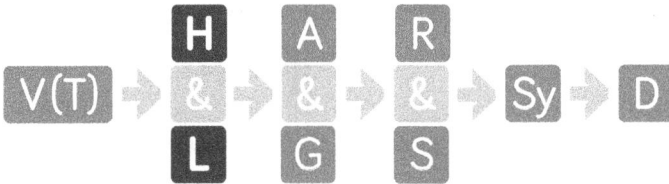

Once I became sufficiently aware of myself, I then realized that after the felt feeling of terror, the first two feelings to surface in my body and mind were hurt and loneliness. At times I may not have been aware of those feelings because my mind tried to step in as quickly as possible to dissociate away those painful feelings. But for any of us, they are always present following each and every felt violation.

Why the hurt and loneliness? We feel hurt (or should) because we have been violated. In fact, we can often feel a stinging sensation in our bodies. We feel some degree of loneliness because, once violated, an unsafe, disconnected, and/or untrustworthy distance has now been created between two individuals.

In addition, if we violate ourselves through poor choices or any particular choice that we decide to be critical of ourselves over, at some level we will experience the same two feelings of hurt and loneliness.

And remember, when I use the word "feel," I am not implying that we are fully aware of those feelings because it is the job of the dissociating capabilities of our mind to block those feelings out. But we are still aware at some level and, as we shall see, the feeling responses from a violation do not go away without a healing or resolution of some sort.

STEP 3: ANGER (A) AND GUILT (G)

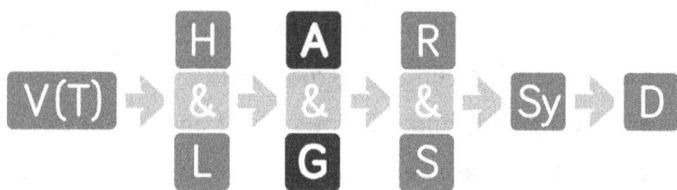

The two feelings of hurt and loneliness are fairly easy to understand. It is when we move past this point that our feelings and emotions become quite confusing, leading to problems in our lives.

If someone violates us, we will first feel the raw feelings of hurt and loneliness, then we will feel an element of anger, again whether or not we are consciously aware of these feelings. Like me, I experienced the anger, but was not consciously aware of it.

Anger is a natural reaction to a felt violation. It is both a healthy and necessary feeling response. We need this felt anger to be able to protect ourselves against a violating world.

Now let me be clear at this point. I am not talking about an angry outburst. That comes under the next heading of "rage." I am referring to the awareness of being able to say to oneself, "I just felt violated and I am feeling some anger. What is that anger about and what do I need to do with that anger? Do I just need to let it go because the incident was not that significant, or do I need to properly address the issue or the person?"

So notice that with such a scenario, the person has the ability to (a) recognize the violation, (b) identify the hurt and/ or loneliness if necessary, (c) identify the corresponding anger, and then (d) make the best and most appropriate choice. In other words, the person is sufficiently in touch with his feelings, and can quietly sit still with himself to calm himself down to use his mind to find the truth of the situation and then act accordingly.

If it is a onetime incident with a person, perhaps the incident can be passed over and/or the person can be forgiven. If it is an ongoing issue, then by addressing the incident with that person, a resolution can hopefully result. And as any of us know, especially in more trusting intimate relationships, we can violate each other quite often unintentionally or accidently. But the sharing of the hurt feelings, and perhaps a little anger (not rage), leads to a healing and a strengthening of relationships.

On the other hand, if the anger is suppressed or denied, then it will eventually cause problems that we will soon get to. Let's now address the other main feeling at this point in the sequence.

Guilt is the feeling we will feel (again whether or not we choose to be consciously aware of it) when we have intentionally or irresponsibly done something to hurt or violate another person. I will shortly explain in detail that shame is quite different than guilt. Quickly defined, shame is the result of another person (or ourselves) trying to make us feel bad or responsible for an action when we have done nothing wrong. It is usually someone else trying to make us feel guilty inappropriately.

Again, true guilt is the resulting feeling when we have irresponsibly hurt or violated another person. But just like anger, if shared appropriately, guilt can be used to mend relationships. If we have done something wrong, we can mend the situation by apologizing and making a commitment to not repeat the same act.

Summary to this point

Our sanity and happiness are highly dependent on the ability to be aware of the "truth feelings" of hurt, loneliness, anger, and guilt, and then to know how to properly address these raw or basic feelings. At times it may take some courage to apologize, or to properly and ideally express our anger. But this is the sanity side of the emotional pain diagram. From this point on, the problems begin, at times even leading all the way to a diagnosis of schizophrenia.

STEP 4: RAGE (R) AND SHAME (S)

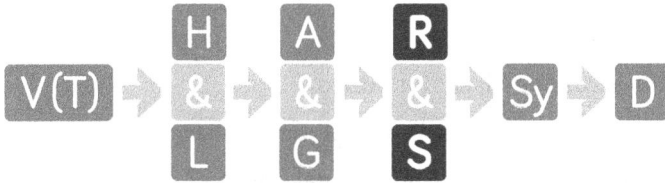

$$V(T) \rightarrow \begin{matrix} H \\ \& \\ L \end{matrix} \rightarrow \begin{matrix} A \\ \& \\ G \end{matrix} \rightarrow \begin{matrix} R \\ \& \\ S \end{matrix} \rightarrow Sy \rightarrow D$$

Again, the feelings of hurt, loneliness, anger, and guilt are what I refer to as raw or pure feeling responses. They are a natural response to felt violations, whether or not we are the violator or the one who has been violated. In their pure form, they have not yet been distorted by our cognitive mind. Thus, for our emotional survival and sanity, we must be able to be aware of these feelings, honor them as a true indication of what just took place, and then make proper decisions accordingly.

But if we do not properly recognize these feelings, or they are too strong to be fully acknowledged and recognized, our mind will step in and begin to emotionalize these raw truth feelings. Instead of feeling angry at someone, our minds may turn that anger into rage as our minds convince us to hate a person, object, or situation.

For example, instead of correctly identifying our truth feelings, we may choose to gossip about a person with an underlying desire to hurt that person and/or his reputation. Yes, gossip can be a form of rage, a very sneaky, mild form, but still rage if it is intended to hurt someone.

Rage can actually take on many forms all the way from vicious kidding, to gossip, to rape and killing. All of this behavior is the result of anger not properly identified, addressed, shared, and/or healed.

Shame is the result of rage or self-hate turned inward at ourselves or when others make us feel guilty when we have done nothing wrong. Shame is an attack upon the selfhood of an individual, not the identification of possible irresponsible behavior.

RAGE AND SHAME—THE MAIN TROUBLEMAKERS

Once again, where hurt, loneliness, anger, and guilt are raw or pure feeling responses, rage and shame are distorted emotional responses. They are the result of our cognitive mind becoming involved and distorting the situation. In fact, a situation or person most likely must be distorted in order to empower or permit the emotions of shame and/or rage. For example, to hate a person to the degree needed to rage at that person, that person usually needs to be seen as more of a villain than he or she may truly be.

In the same sense, when we shame or damn ourselves, we are usually distorting who we are as a person. For example, I ran groups in prison for men who had been sexually abused as children, most often by someone they knew and trusted or needed to trust. Consequently, they suffered tremendously from the emotions of both rage and shame. As a result, they had been in and out of prison for most of their adult lives. They were usually arrested either for violent crimes or illegal drug involvement.

The act of incest results in an overwhelming amount of hurt, loneliness, and anger. The anger turns into a rage because, when anyone has been violated, there is a corresponding desire or need to get even or hurt back. If we can't hurt the person who hurt us, then in a distorted way, we can attempt to regain a sense of dignity, respect, and power by violating someone else. And again, when that anger is suppressed, our mind often takes over and eventually turns it into a form of rage.

In terms of incest, the shame is also immense and overpowering because a trusting adult has violated and used the body of a child for his or her own pleasure. And in fact, the prison incest survivors were constantly haunted with a "Why me?" shaming message. "Why did that person make me do those acts? What was wrong or bad about me?"

Since the child was not doing anything wrong, feelings of guilt would not be appropriate. So the raw feelings were then transformed into shame and/or rage.

It is also important to note that there may be several reasons that a person's mind will emotionalize an event, resulting in the distorted emotions of rage and shame. Again, when the violating event took place, that person felt overwhelmed with the raw feelings of hurt and loneliness. In addition, even though the rage and shame are painful emotions, they are less painful than the raw feelings of hurt and loneliness. With hurt and loneliness, we are left powerless and at the mercy of those feelings. Rage and shame give us a chance to avoid these primary feelings as well as give us at least a superficial or momentary sense of control and power.

With shame, for example, a child can believe that by punishing himself, he will become a better child and thus the violators (i.e., his parents) will now love him or change their behavior. Rage, of course, is seductive because, when in a state of rage, a person feels extremely powerful.

Quick summary

So it is the violation of our selfhood and the corresponding terror that sets off the sequence. The feelings of hurt, loneliness, anger, and guilt, if identified properly, are undistorted feelings and tell us the truth about a situation. If someone has violated us, we will experience anger. If we have violated someone else, we will experience guilt, whether or not we have the desire, courage, or ability to be fully aware of these guilt feelings.

Rage and shame are the result of these basic "truth feelings" distorted by our minds for a particular purpose, either to justify hurting others, empowering ourselves, or punishing ourselves. Where guilt provides us with the opportunity to make amends, rage and shame attempt to destroy others and/or ourselves.

EMERGING SYMPTOMS (SY) AND EVENTUAL DIAGNOSES (D)

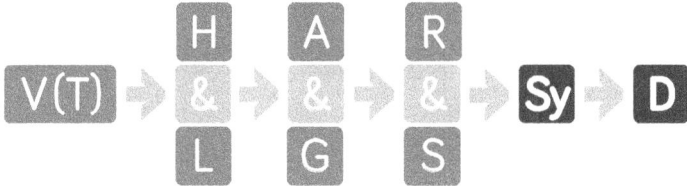

The major psychiatric diagnoses, mainly depression, mania, schizophrenia, and paranoia, are the result of unhealed violations. Most of us have heard the saying that depression is anger turned inward. Actually, the dissociation of any painful feeling over time can result in a depressive condition or state of mind.

Mania, on the other hand, is the result of the mind speeding up, often in an optimistic way, to help the person dissociate or stay away from the painful feelings. Read how the late actress Patty Duke described the purpose (intentionality) behind her manic episodes.

> That's the childlike part of the mania. It's whatever you see you want, that's it, it's yours, with no thought, not the slightest anxiety about what it takes to get it or how you're going to pay for it. It really is like believing that the money's all growing on trees. During mania, we own the world, we don't need anybody, and we don't need anything. We're going to be millionaires, and we believe it.[1]

Schizophrenia, or psychosis, in its most elementary form is simply the mind splitting from a present reality in a more desperate attempt to avoid these painful feelings. This, of course, is an oversimplified explanation, but one that will do for now. Nevertheless, the following is a quote from one professional, Jack Rosberg, who spent much of his life traveling the world, teaching other professionals the true nature of schizophrenia.

> I wish to explain how schizophrenia becomes a lifestyle. In the initial phase of schizophrenia, the early onset is a terror syndrome. There is a dissolution of identity and the patient not only feels lost, but also is terrified of destruction and has a feeling of nothingness about him/herself. He/she hangs between life and death and in desperation, retreating to a place where they are able to organize around themselves, a series of workable defenses. The fear is processed into symptoms which reduce the anxiety and they feel a sense of greater security; so one can see that schizophrenia is a survival system with its own logic and language. It has purpose. It has meaning. Those individuals, who suffer from that condition, are not completely comfortable, but feel much relief. So that's what we had to deal with: patients who had found a way of surviving in a world that they perceived as a threat to their lives.[2]

Again, the more severe forms of what are referred to as "mental illness" are, in one way or another, that person's response to terror and the suppression of the corresponding feelings.

WHEN AND WHERE FEELINGS AND EMOTIONS BEGIN TO CAUSE SERIOUS PROBLEMS

Once again, the key to proper mental health is to have the ability to recognize when a violation has taken place by others or ourselves and then to act accordingly.

In the most simplistic form, when violated, we can best approach a situation by using what is referred to as "I" statements. For example, "I feel hurt and angry when you ..." (specific behavior).

Notice in this example, the person is starting with the raw, pure feelings of hurt and anger and then addressing the other person's behavior, rather than attacking the person.

Again, with guilt, making amends for irresponsible behavior properly heals the situation or relationship.

The problem that eventually results in the major forms of a so-called mental illness begins when a person becomes confused about his or her emotions. Some individuals will tend to feel guilty for almost anything they do, saying "sorry" at the hint of any possible wrongdoing. Of course, quickly apologizing can be a way of attempting to neutralize the other person, but it further leaves the "feeling sorry" person helpless in the long run to take care of him or herself.

Other individuals, at the instant of feeling any element of pain, including guilt, will quickly turn that pain into rage. Even a nasty stare back is a form of rage. Why? Because it is intended to be an attack upon the other person.

As a person develops the habit of using shame (or false guilt) to avoid deeper, more painful feelings, that person will gradually emotionally chip away at himself instead of taking care of himself.

It is at this point that forms of paranoia and possibly fictitious voices are created by the subconscious mind in an attempt to help the person out. It is as if the person is now so disconnected from his raw truth feelings that his mind must come to his rescue. That's why, if a helper takes the time to understand the content of the paranoia and/or the voices, these behaviors will be attached to very specific feelings and circumstances.

For example, I had one inmate who, when he would begin to feel extremely discouraged, would hear the voice of his affirming grandmother who raised him. He would not hear just any person's voice. He would hear *her* encouraging voice.

I had another client who would sit at a specific street corner, hour after hour, waiting for her children. Years before, her ex-husband was able to legally take her children away from her. He then moved across the country where, because of her finances, she was unable to see them. She believed that they would return to this corner someday because it was her mind's best and perhaps only way of giving her a sense of hope and a reason to live.

Rage and shame—out of control

Once again, the feelings of hurt, loneliness, anger, and guilt are what I refer to as *truth* feelings. They will result from a felt violation independent of the person's mind distorting or emotionalizing the event or situations. But once the mind begins to transform these raw feelings into the emotions of rage and shame, a corresponding loss of reality results. In fact, the emotions of rage and shame can build upon each other. Let me first start with rage.

When a person rages at another person, he violates that person, not necessarily because of what that person did, but because of the raging person's suppressed feelings and distorting mind. Thus the raging act is an improper display of anger and, at some level, the raging person will experience some true guilt. But because that person is perhaps already overloaded with suppressed unresolved and unhealed painful feelings, that person will not be able to address his or her true guilt. In fact, the added true guilt may make the person feel even more out of control wherein that person will need to blame the other person even more, resulting in more rage.

It is generally assumed in my profession that serial killers and rapists, or individuals with sociopathic personalities, don't feel any guilt. That is not true. They feel it, but since they already have an overwhelming amount of unresolved guilt, their minds quickly come to their rescue by turning the guilt into more rage.

Thus, as a serial killer justifies the killing of a person, he will be hit with a sudden overload of guilt. But that guilt will quickly and almost instantaneously be turned into more rage by his emotionalizing mind. That is why, with serial killers and rapists, the time between each event often becomes shorter and shorter. Their minds have to create more and more rage to cover up or suppress their growing amount of guilt.

I know this sequence firsthand because, as I have stated before, I have a problem with anger. At times when I have become unfairly angry at my wife, I have felt an overwhelming amount of true guilt afterwards. The guilt can become so intense that my mind will then attempt to come to my rescue by looking for another reason to be angry at my wife. But by understanding this scenario, and after properly addressing the particular situation, the true guilt-to-rage transfer disappears. Yet for some individuals who are out of control with their rage, the felt guilt will then set off more rage. In fact, I believe some of the most severe abusive situations are the result of true guilt turned into additional rage.

That is the rage side of the entrapment. What about the shame side that is much more responsible for creating symptoms referred to as mental illness? This is because rage empowers the individual, whereas shame weakens the individual.

Remember, shame is the result of others (at times ourselves) convincing us that we have done something wrong, or that we are bad or no good, when we have done nothing wrong. It is an attack upon who we are, our being, or for just being alive versus any irresponsible behavior. It is being told that we are less than okay, not loveable or worthwhile because of our looks, nationality, or because of some event like a child accidently spilling his milk.

Since the person did not commit any wrongful act, at least not intentionally, the person is helpless to defend himself when accused by an authority figure who has a certain degree of power over him. If a child accidently spills his milk and is told he is "no good" or "stupid" or "clumsy," how does that child change such a so-called defect? If a kid is teased for his big ears, what does he do with the resulting feelings? If he does not have the power to overcome such a violation, he will begin to hate himself (or others). Thus, for the kid who is teased for his big ears, his only choice is to either rage back at others or shame himself. Until someone is strong enough to overcome such violations, a person's mind will be forced to emotionalize the situation, changing the raw truth feelings into either rage or shame, or eventually splitting from reality.

Thus, for the person with a serious mental or emotional condition, I can guarantee that his or her life is filled with suppressed feelings of shame and/or rage. In fact, if that person is mostly aware of his or her shame, there will be a corresponding amount of rage underneath. For the person who is quick to rage, there will be a corresponding amount of shame because, as he rages, he has also shamed himself.

BACK TO THE OTHER FEELINGS

I want to spend some extra time on the emotions of rage and shame because they are often misunderstood by my profession. But the unresolved feelings of hurt and loneliness can also cause major problems leading all the way to the creation of voices and then, of course, a possible diagnosis of schizophrenia or psychosis.

One of the clearest cases was that of a very lonely woman who lived by herself and eventually began to hear the TV talking to her. Once I got her back involved with people outside of her home, such as attending church and joining a senior citizens group, the voices disappeared. But as I think back about this case that took place over 30 years ago, I now recognize the shame that she felt, believing no one wanted to be with her. So, getting her involved solved the problem of both her loneliness and her shame. In addition, because of her shame, she was allowing a couple of relatives to take advantage of her. Thus, once she felt the acceptance (and love) of people from her church, and with some therapy, she became strong enough to defend herself against these predators.

WHAT ABOUT BIOLOGICAL POSSIBILITIES?

Notice that I have not mentioned anything about possible biological issues such as defective genes or chemical imbalances. That is because it is finally being admitted by many highly respected professionals that no such defects exist. In reference to a possible chemical imbalance, neuroscientist Steven Hyman, past director of the National Institute of Mental Health, has stated that psychotropic drugs are similar to drugs of abuse (street drugs), in that they work by disabling the brain.[3] In other words, they work by suppressing a person's emotions and thoughts. More recently, Jan Olav Johannessen, chair of the 55-year-old international professional organization, The International Society for Psychological and Social Approaches to Psychosis, stated, "I think it is fair to state that the search for the schizophrenic gene has failed."[4] Such a lack of findings exists for the other major disorders as well.

On the other hand, medical or physical conditions such as certain handicaps, appearances, painful body ailments, etc., can add to the picture when they are added to the person's painful feelings. Personality characteristics may also help to explain some behaviors. Some personalities may be more inclined to turn hurt and loneliness into rage versus shame. But it is still the felt violation and corresponding terror that is the true source of the problem.

HEALING AND RECOVERY

Let me just say a few words about the healing and recovery process because this is obviously a huge and often complicated topic in and of itself.

Next you will find a diagram showing an approximation of the various basic therapeutic processes while illustrating the emotional pain sequence at the top.

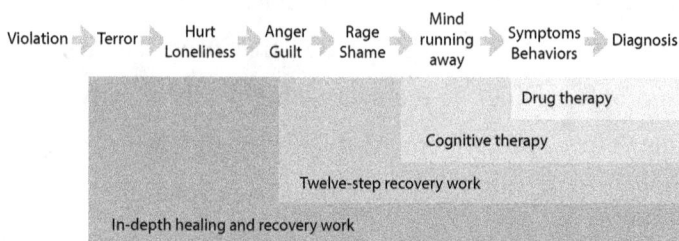

Violation	Terror	Hurt Loneliness	Anger Guilt	Rage Shame	Mind running away	Symptoms Behaviors	Diagnosis
						Drug therapy	
					Cognitive therapy		
				Twelve-step recovery work			
	In-depth healing and recovery work						

Let me quickly go through each of them.

DRUG THERAPY

Again, it is now fully admitted that these drugs do not correct a chemical imbalance. Instead, they act much like street drugs or drugs of abuse. They disable the brain so that the person does not experience the pain of the violating events to their fullest intensity, and often not at all. They work much the same as the father having a few drinks of alcohol at night to block out the pain of a violating day. Thus, they may work for a while, but eventually the underlying events and feelings must be identified and approached in one way or another.

Caution: Do not use this material as permission to suddenly stop the use of psychotropic drugs without proper medical advice. The withdrawal of some of these substances can become life threatening.

COGNITIVE THERAPY

As I have explained, these painful feelings can and will set off a person's mind to the degree that the mind will begin to distort the situation. Remember, because I was blocked out from my anger, when I was challenged in that class at USC, I thought everyone else was wrong and that they were out to get me for some reason. (I am exaggerating this second part but my mind was searching for a reason for their "unexplainable" conclusions.)

Luckily, the eventual awareness of my truth feelings straightened my mind out. But what about the person who cannot get in touch with his or her truth feelings for one reason or another? Cognitive therapy or some form of rational reasoning may be the best way to start the healing, recovery, and truth-seeking process.

This, of course, is an oversimplified explanation of cognitive therapy. But in its basic form, cognitive therapy starts with the mind's distorted thoughts and proceeds from that point.

TWELVE-STEP RECOVERY WORK

Because of unresolved and unhealed painful feelings, a person may develop certain out-of-control or addictive behaviors such as drug abuse, inappropriate eating patterns, excessive spending and so forth. Twelve-step programs help tremendously with such possible destructive behaviors.

IN-DEPTH HEALING AND GRIEF WORK

Here is how I like to explain the need for this kind of therapy. Assume that you have a young daughter, say age nine, who had been kidnapped for a few days and was sexually abused. How would you go about ideally helping her?

Would you give her a drug to quiet or suppress her symptoms and be satisfied with that solution? No! Through the help of a doctor, you might have her prescribed a sleeping pill, but hopefully you would not be satisfied with that solution alone.

Most likely you would spend a lot of time with her, holding her as she relived this terrible time, possibly crying in the process and/or letting out some anger. In addition, if she was having problems sleeping at night, you would probably have one parent either be with her or have her stay in your bedroom. In any case, your main goal would be to address her deeper pain until a corresponding healing resulted.

One of the major events that affected psychiatrist Frieda Fromm-Reichman's view of mental illness and her eventual successful treatment of schizophrenia was the extremely low incidence of psychiatric symptoms among civilian victims of the Blitz (the constant bombing of London by Germany in World War II). Quoting from her biography,

> A few people had needed sedation for brief periods, but if they were brought to a mobile unit right after the bombing and encouraged to express their feelings, even these victims had recovered

"immediately and completely, no matter how severe the actual incident had been." Chronic disturbances occurred among people unable to verbalize their terror.... Therefore, it couldn't be the trauma itself that produced mental illness; it had to be the repression of the trauma.[5]

Thus, in-depth healing can take place shortly after a violating incident or much later. The problem with in-depth healing is that it often takes an extra skilled and committed therapist to do this type of work. In-depth healing work can bring up a lot of strong, distorted feelings that may also scare and/or trigger similar feelings in the therapist or helper. Unfortunately, when such a situation occurs, the therapist or helper often inappropriately turns to medication and/or an inappropriate dependency on cognitive forms of therapy. The pain must come up, be revisited and healed by the affirmation of another person. Just remember what the young abused girl needed.

SUMMARY DIAGRAM OF THE HEALING PROCESS

Below you will find a diagram depicting the basic overall healing process from the trauma to the meaningful protective behavior and back to the trauma.

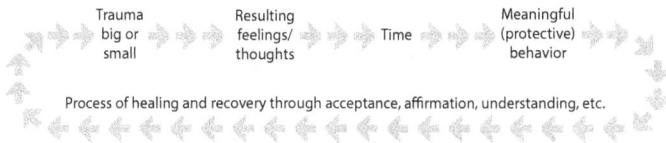

Trauma big or small ⟹ Resulting feelings/ thoughts ⟹ Time ⟹ Meaningful (protective) behavior ⟹

Process of healing and recovery through acceptance, affirmation, understanding, etc.

Notice that I have inserted "meaningful (protective) behavior" in place of the usual "mental illness diagnoses." The behavior may not be externally productive for the individual (job, relationships, etc.), but it is still there for a purpose. Excessive drinking certainly can become a problem, but it was originally used to help suppress painful, unresolved feelings.

AN EVERYDAY COMMON EXAMPLE

It is important to realize that I am also describing behavior that is quite common. Here is an example that took place as I was in the process of writing this booklet.

Besides being a psychologist, I spent a few years coaching at the high school level, and also received a certificate in sports psychology. At a gym that I often attended, I sometimes noticed how the trainers inappropriately attempted to instruct their clients. The technical aspect was fine, but the trainers often took a new client and asked the person to do exercises that were too difficult and embarrassing to do in front of other gym members. When I saw this, I said to myself, "This person is not returning," and I was usually right.

I finally decided to approach the manager in the most non-threatening way that I could because I figured that he had received a lot of complaints anyway. I really did not want to make a complaint. I simply wanted the place to become more successful and to help people.

As I started to gently explain what I was observing, I could immediately sense a protective wall go up. I then took an even more gentle approach, trying to make sure he knew I wasn't complaining, but just wanted to help.

But as I continued, I could sense the surfacing of some shame (or guilt if he knew that their teaching style was inappropriate). Below his shame, I could also sense some fear (terror) on his face. But within an instant, his shame or guilt switched to a mild form of anger. His anger was so slight that it came across more as a defensive wall. But instead of letting down his guard and listening to me, I could tell that he was slightly irritated by my message and thus me. He did say, "Thanks," but at the same time, he also made some poor excuses.

This was a small incident, but it was a great example because we all can become "guilty" of such behaviors when a painful situation arises. Yet, again, it is important to realize that it is this same everyday common behavior that, under certain conditions, can lead to what we refer to as major forms of "mental Illness."

Regardless of whether the therapeutic process is started from a feeling or cognitive level, it is the rejoining and resolution of these two aspects of our lives that result in a proper healing and recovery process. Where drugs attempt to work by maintaining the separation between the violated feelings and a person's thoughts or beliefs, a true healing and recovery program heals either by approaching from a cognitive perspective or an inner healing-feeling perspective.

This same process takes place between, let's say the manager above, or me, and a person who eventually is diagnosed with schizophrenia. The only difference is in the magnitude of the felt violations and the person's need to dissociate off the resulting painful feelings and then create a new and hopefully safer way to relate to others and the world. But isn't that how we all operate at times when emotionally threatened?

THE USE OF STICK FIGURE ILLUSTRATIONS

To help suffering individuals better understand the relationships between their painful feelings and their out-of-control, runaway minds, as well as any corresponding non-productive behavior, I often use a stick figure diagram to give the person a visual illustration. The following figure represents the basic diagram that I usually start with. The explanation of this diagram will also act as a review of the emotional process from a violating experience to distorted emotions and thoughts. When I do present this material to a person, I usually draw out the diagram on a sheet of paper and then provide information that may be relevant to that particular person (i.e., the kind of thoughts and/or feelings that may be most prevalent to that person).

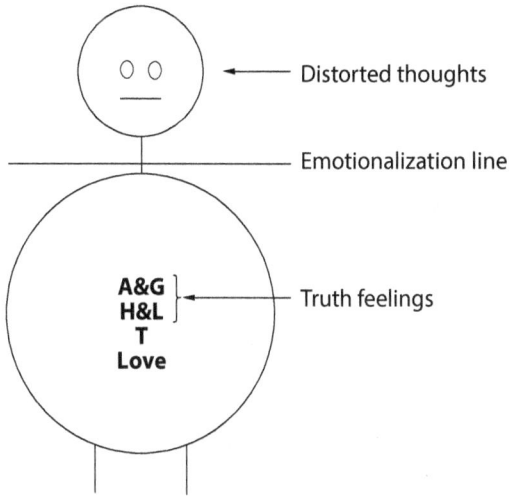

As depicted by the diagram above, the feelings of hurt, loneliness, anger, and guilt represent the true or undistorted awareness of a particular violating moment or situation. Notice also that once our minds engage, we begin to transform these "truth" feelings into distorted thoughts.

What I need to make note of at this juncture, and what I often point out to clients, is that we stockpile or suppress our feelings in a particular order. Let me explain.

As depicted by the above diagram, our need to be loved as well as to possess the potential to give love is often suppressed at the deepest level. The more someone has been unfairly violated, especially as a child, the more his or her love ability to give and receive love must be suppressed, covered up, disguised (perhaps through the manipulation of others), or protected from further harm.

This is because, as conscious human beings, our need to give and receive love represents the most vulnerable and unprotected part of our selfhood. After all, to truly love and be loved, we must attempt to void ourselves of all possible resistance or protection.

In reality, our need to love and be loved has most likely split into different parts depending on past experiences. For example, a person who has difficulty forming a quality and trusting romantic relationship because of past violating experiences may still be quite capable of properly loving and caring for children. And, of course, the opposite can be true.

Next in line, through the process of denial and/or dissociation, our mind attempts to suppress the terror associated with violating conditions that felt overwhelming at the time. The awareness of terror is then followed by the four truth feelings. Also, as depicted by the diagram, shame and rage are shown above the "emotionalization line" because they are emotions (versus pure feelings) that have been transformed or distorted by our mind.

The diagram below shows an expanded view of the process.

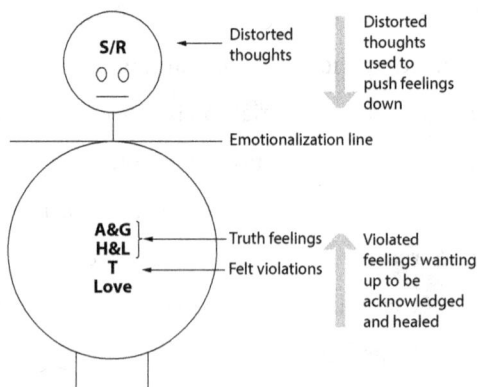

How to use these stick figure diagrams

I am sure that some individuals may struggle against how I have so "precisely" depicted the above process. But accuracy is not as important as helping to give the suffering person and his or her helpers an overall view of the problem and the therapeutic work that may need to take place.

Sometimes just addressing a person's distorted or overly emotionalized thoughts is sufficient. I can't tell you how many times I, my wife, or my children have come home from a violating day and just needed someone to be a compassionate listener and/or offer some simple but valuable feedback.

But in more severe violating situations, especially if they occurred sometime in the past, the healing and recovery process must start from a person's non-productive behavior and/or thoughts, then travel down through the shame or rage, then to the anger and/or guilt and so forth. Let's look at a simplified example to illustrate this sequence.

My parents had been married for 62 years when my father passed away. My mother was, of course, saddened by his passing. But like most individuals of their generation, she never felt that comfortable sharing her deeper emotional pain.

A few days after the funeral, I happened to ask my mother how she was doing. She responded with a quick "okay" because, on a cognitive level, she was doing fine. She was in good health, financially secure, and had plenty of people who loved her and were available for her.

Then, with a more serious tone to my voice, I again asked her, "How are you really doing?" At that point she broke down crying, telling me that she was afraid to be alone. Now, at such an emotionally vulnerable place, she allowed me to give her a big, reassuring hug.

She also then told me that she felt guilty (shameful) sharing her needs when others were also hurting (a true mother).

So, in that quick moment, we were able to travel from her cognitive distorted mind ("I am okay") to the shame of sharing or even having her own feelings, down to her hurt and loneliness and finally to her terror about being alone.

Once we had penetrated through her minefield of emotions and feelings, she was now able to better accept my love.

Also, by keeping her painful feelings suppressed, several different forms of a so-called mental illness could and probably would have eventually emerged. Depression and different forms of anxiety would not be a surprising outcome. But it is also not uncommon for extremely isolated seniors to become delusional, paranoid, and even begin to hallucinate.

The next example that I often use involved my work with the inmates who had been sexually abused as children. Again, as a result of the hurt and loneliness that they experienced, as well as the shame that often turned into a vicious rage, they had been in and out of prison for the vast majority of their adult lives.

Furthermore, most of them had been diagnosed with a major mental illness, including schizophrenia. In fact, if in the original interview, an inmate told me he had been in and out of prison many times and had been given a diagnosis of schizophrenia, I would then ask him if he had been sexually abused. These inmates answered with a "Yes" about 80% of the time. (So, his diagnosis should have been a "victim of extreme trauma," not schizophrenia.)

Many of them had been diagnosed with schizophrenia because of how hard their minds were having to race, distorting reality, becoming overly protective (paranoid), and often creating voices, all to keep them away from full awareness of their emotional pain. I am sure anyone can at least begin to imagine the terror that these individuals must have felt as a young child in the process of being raped or forced into oral sex most often by a trusted adult.

To help them unravel the confusion surrounding their feelings and emotions, I would often quickly draw a stick figure diagram to help them better understand their feelings, emotions, and distorted thoughts. Such an understanding would help them to identify their deeper pain, and then share it with others in the safety of the group.

As a result, at times the whole group of seven or eight men, including myself, would be in tears after one of the inmates had shared from his deepest place of vulnerability. The diagram would also help them to begin identifying which feelings and emotions were appropriate for the situation and which ones were not. For example, some of them felt a lot of shame (or false guilt) believing that in some way, they must have been at least partially responsible for the abuse.

After being in and out of prison for most of their adult lives, and after sharing at their deepest level, these men were not returning to prison. I had a couple of inmates who had been in prison over 20 times, but were never given a chance to share this pain with anyone, even after being under the care of several mental health professionals.

I did not need to draw out a stick figure diagram for my mother, but they were very helpful at times with the inmates. Instead of simply giving them a diagnosis of some kind and then medicating (actually drugging) them, a stick figure diagram helped them to visualize the overall process and then take responsibility for their lives.

HOW AND WHERE TO START THE THERAPEUTIC HEALING AND RECOVERY PROCESS

The following diagram helps to visualize where to start the healing and recovery process. It is an oversimplified explanation, but it does help to put the overall process in perspective.

Mind racing
out of control

S/R

O O

Best to start here when the
mind is too out of control
and the person is not ready
to experience strong
feelings—and may even
need a drug to help

Overwhelming
feelings

**A&G
H&L
T
Love**

Best when the person is more
in control of his/her mind and
able to face the violating
feelings—drugs usually
impede this process

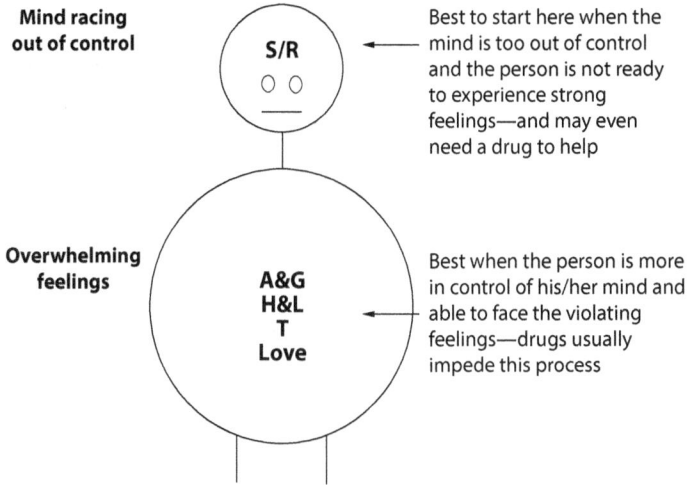

The method or approach used is certainly dependent
upon the needs and personality of the suffering person, as well
as the experience and skills of the helpers. I much prefer to
work on a deeper, inner healing-feeling basis, but some clients
just do better from a more cognitive approach.

The incest survivors in the prison who made the most
progress used different forms of cognitive therapy or assistance
(religious beliefs, affirmations, etc.), and were involved
in 12-step meetings. In addition, they were participating in
deeper feeling-inner healing work with me.

SUMMARY

On the next page you will find another stick figure diagram
that summarizes the overall process.

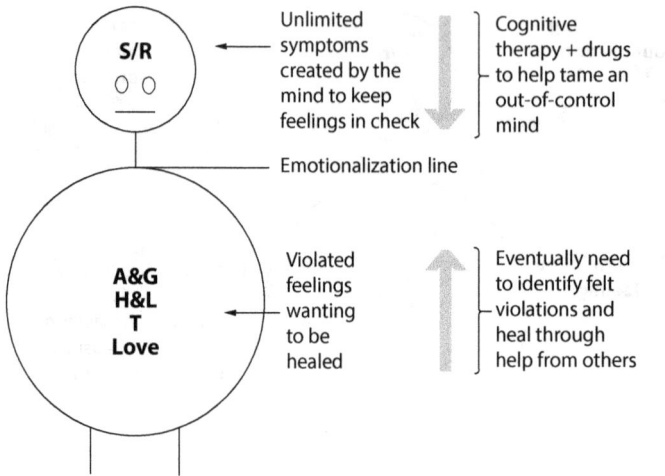

Unlimited symptoms created by the mind to keep feelings in check

S/R
O O

Cognitive therapy + drugs to help tame an out-of-control mind

Emotionalization line

A&G
H&L
T
Love

Violated feelings wanting to be healed

Eventually need to identify felt violations and heal through help from others

Notice that from the cognitive or mental side (above the emotionalization line), I have added the possibility of the use of psychotropic medications. But once more, it has now been admitted by the NIMH that these drugs work by disabling the brain, thus helping to cut off the person from his or her deeper felt violated feelings. Consequently, the use of these substances may eventually limit the emotional healing that needs to take place.

On the other hand, if the mind is running away so fast that it puts the person in danger (destructive behavior) or the person is unable to focus at all on the therapeutic process, then perhaps some assistance may be needed with the eventual hope of removing (*under proper supervision*) these toxic substances.

FURTHER STUDY

For a more in-depth explanation of the Emotional Pain Diagram and how it relates to problems in mental health, refer to my book, *Healing Runaway Minds*.

REFERENCES

1. P. Duke and H. Gloria, *A Brilliant Madness* (New Y o r k : Bantam, 1992), p. 9.

2. J. Rosberg, "Molde, Norway Revisited," Schizophrenia. net (June 1999), retrieved April 19, 2013, from www. schizophreniarecovery.net/newsletter/jun99.htm.

3. S.E. Hyman and E. J. Nestler, *"Initiation and Adaptation: A Paradigm for Understanding Psychotropic Drug Action,"* American Journal of Psychiatry, Vol. 153, No. 2 (February 1996), pp. 151–162.

4. J. O. Johannessen, email (November 16, 2915), jan.olav. johannessen@sus.no.

5. G. A. Hornstein, *To Redeem One Person Is to Redeem the World* (New York: Other Press, 2000), p. 123.

www.ingramcontent.com/pod-product-compliance
Lightning Source LLC
Chambersburg PA
CBHW060657280326
41933CB00012B/2222